ICH ESSE GERNE OBST UND GEMÜSE
I LOVE TO EAT FRUITS AND VEGETABLES

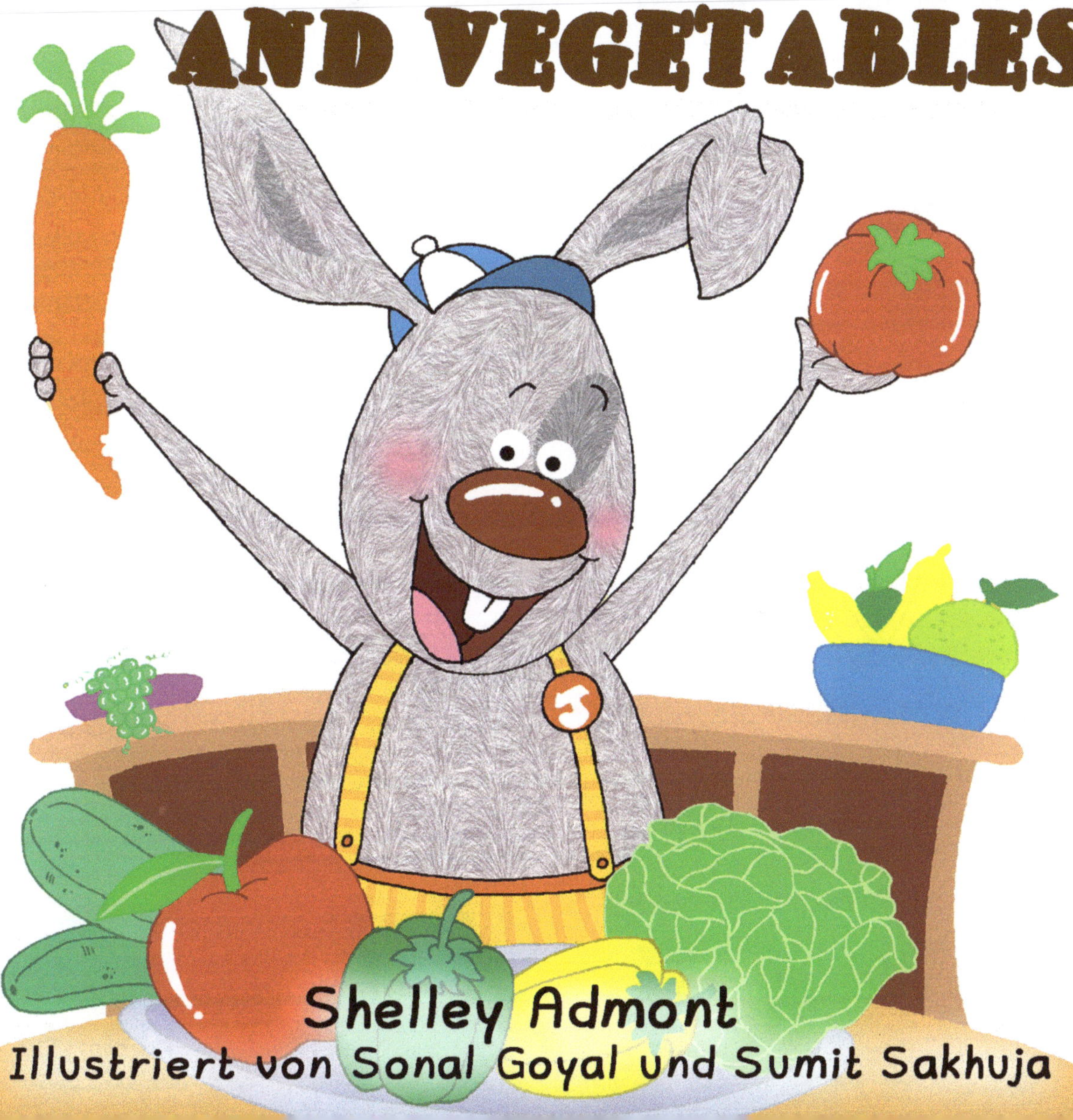

Shelley Admont
Illustriert von Sonal Goyal und Sumit Sakhuja

www.kidkiddos.com
Copyright©2014 by S.A.Publishing ©2017 by KidKiddos Books Ltd.
support@kidkiddos.com

All rights reserved. No part of this book may be reproduced in any form or by any electronic or mechanical means, including information storage and retrieval systems, without written permission from the publisher or author, except in the case of a reviewer, who may quote brief passages embodied in critical articles or in a review.

Alle Rechte vorbehalten. Kein Teil dieses Buches darf in irgendeiner Form oder durch irgendwelche elektronischen oder mechanischen Mitteln, einschließlich Informationen Regalbediengeräte schriftlich beim Verlag, mit Ausnahme von einem Rezensenten, kurze Passagen in einer Bewertung zitieren darf reproduziert, ohne Erlaubnis.
Second edition, 2019

Translated from English by Tess Parthum
Aus dem Englischen übersetzt von Tess Parthum

Library and Archives Canada Cataloguing in Publication
I love to eat fruits and vegetables (German English Bilingual Edition)/ Shelley Admont
ISBN: 978-1-5259-1639-7 paperback
ISBN: 978-1-77268-581-7 hardcover
ISBN: 978-1-77268-258-8 ebook

Please note that the German and English versions of the story have been written to be as close as possible. However, in some cases they differ in order to accommodate nuances and fluidity of each language.

KidKiddos Books

Für die, die ich am meisten liebe – S.A.

For those I love the most – S.A.

Es war eine Stunde vor dem Mittagessen. Jimmy, ein kleiner Hase, spielte gerade mit seinen beiden älteren Brüdern.
It was an hour before lunch. Jimmy, a little bunny, was playing with his two older brothers.

„Ich habe wirklich Lust, etwas Süßes zu essen", sagte Jimmy plötzlich. „Vielleicht hat Mama einen Lolli oder ein Stück Schokolade für uns."
"I really feel like eating something sweet," said Jimmy suddenly. "Maybe Mom has a lollipop or a piece of chocolate with raisins for us."

„Wir können keine Süßigkeiten vor dem Mittag essen", sagte der älteste Bruder. „Du weißt, dass wir das nicht dürfen, Jimmy."
"We can't eat candy before lunch," said the oldest brother. "You know we're not allowed, Jimmy."

„Ich mag Äpfel und Trauben", sagte der mittlere Bruder. „Sie sind süß und lecker."

"I like apples and grapes," said the middle brother. "They're sweet and tasty."

Jimmy verzog den Mund. „Igitt, ich esse nicht gerne Obst." Dann flüsterte er: „Wisst ihr was? Ich habe gesehen, dass Mama gestern neue Süßigkeiten gekauft hat. Ich werde mir welche holen. Wer kommt mit?"

Jimmy curled his lip. "Yuck, I don't like eating fruits." Then he whispered, "Guess what? I saw that Mom bought some new candy yesterday. I'm going to take some. Who's joining me?"

„Ich nicht", sagte der älteste Bruder und ging zurück zu seinen Spielsachen.

"Not me," said his oldest brother and went back to his toys.

„Ich komme auch nicht mit", antwortete der mittlere Bruder.

"I'm not coming either," replied his middle brother.

Jimmy winkte ihnen zu und verließ das Zimmer. Langsam ging er in die Küche und schaute sich um, ob ihn auch niemand beobachtete.

Jimmy waved his hand and left the room. Slowly, he made his way to the kitchen, looking around to check that nobody was watching.

Der Tisch war bereits für das Mittagessen vorbereitet.

The table was already prepared for lunch.

Jeder Hase hatte seinen eigenen Teller. Der älteste Bruder hatte den blauen Teller und der mittlere den grünen. Der orange Teller war für Jimmy.

Each bunny had his own plate. The oldest brother had the blue plate, and the middle brother had the green one. The orange plate was for Jimmy.

In der Mitte des Tisches war eine große, mit frischem Gemüse gefüllte Schüssel. Es gab Gurken, Karotten, Tomaten, rote und gelbe Paprikas und etwas Kohl.

In the center of the table was a big bowl filled with fresh vegetables. There were cucumbers, carrots, tomatoes, red and yellow peppers, and some cabbage.

Jimmy rümpfte die Nase. Pfui! DAS werde ich nicht essen, dachte er.

Jimmy scrunched his nose. Ugh! I'm not going to eat THAT, he thought.

Er ging hinüber zum Schrank und entdeckte die Tüte mit Süßigkeiten. Aber der Schrank war so hoch, dass Jimmy sie nicht erreichen konnte.

He went over to the cupboard and spotted the bag of candy. But the cupboard was so high that Jimmy was unable to reach it.

Er nahm einen der Stühle und schob ihn näher an den Schrank heran. Er kletterte darauf, aber er kam immer noch nicht an das Regal heran!

He took one of the chairs and moved it nearer to the cupboard. He climbed up onto it, but he still wasn't able to reach the shelf!

Jimmy stieg wieder herunter und schaute sich nochmal um. Diesmal nahm er einen großen, leeren Topf und drehte ihn um. Er legte den Topf auf den Stuhl und kletterte hinauf.

Jimmy got back down and looked around again. This time, he took a large empty pot and turned it upside down. He put the pot on the chair and then climbed up.

Jetzt konnte er das höchste Regal sehen. In der hintersten Ecke war eine riesige Tüte voll mit Naschereien!

Now, he was able to see the highest shelf. In the far corner of the shelf, there it was a huge bag full of candy!

Doch...er konnte sie immer noch nicht ergreifen. Er musste noch ein winziges Stück höher kommen.

But... he still wasn't able to touch it. He needed to be a tiny bit higher.

Was kann ich noch benutzen? dachte Jimmy, während er hinunterstieg. Plötzlich sah er Mamas großes Kochbuch. „Das ist genau das, was ich brauche!", rief er fröhlich und schnappte sich das Buch.

What else can I use? thought Jimmy while getting down. He saw his mom's huge cookbook. "That's exactly what I need!" he said happily as he grabbed the book.

Er legte das Kochbuch auf den Topf, der verkehrt herum auf dem Stuhl lag, und kletterte langsam hinauf.

He put the cookbook on the upside-down pot and again started slowly climbing up.

Doch als Jimmy nach der Tüte mit Süßigkeiten fasste, begann der Stuhl zu wackeln. Jimmy verlor sein Gleichgewicht und fiel flach auf den Boden.

But as Jimmy reached for the bag of candy, the chair began to rock. Jimmy quickly lost his balance and fell flat on the ground.

Der Topf fiel mit einem lauten Knall neben ihn. Das Kochbuch kam als nächstes und landete genau auf dem Kopf des armen Jimmy.

The pot fell next to him with a loud bang. The cookbook came next, and it landed right on poor Jimmy's head.

Jimmy schaute hinauf zum Schrank und er schien höher und höher zu werden. Als er versuchte, aufzustehen, wurde ihm noch schummriger und er musste sich wieder setzen.

Jimmy looked up at the cupboard and it seemed as if it was getting higher and higher. When he tried to stand up on his feet, he felt dizzier and had to sit back down.

Jimmy winkte. „Ich bin hier!"
Jimmy waved his hand. "I'm here!"

„Jimmy, du siehst...anders aus", sagte der älteste Bruder.
„Wie bist du so winzig geworden?", fragte sein mittlerer Bruder.
"Jimmy, you look...different," said the oldest brother.
"How did you get so tiny?" asked his middle brother.

Erst jetzt begriff Jimmy, warum alles so groß aussah. Er war so klein wie eine Maus geworden!
Now, Jimmy understood why everything looked so big. He had become as small as a mouse!

„Ich bin nur hochgeklettert, um mir Süßigkeiten zu nehmen", rief er, „und dann bin ich runtergefallen."
"I just climbed up to get some candy," he cried, "and then I fell down."

„Vielleicht bist du deshalb so klein geworden!", rief der mittlere Bruder.
"Maybe that's what caused you to become so little!" exclaimed the middle brother.

„Oh nein. Werde ich für immer so klein bleiben?" Jimmy fing an zu weinen.
"Oh, no! Will I stay this small forever?" Jimmy screamed and began crying hard.

„Weine nicht", sagte der älteste Bruder. „Wir lassen uns etwas einfallen. Lasst uns erstmal aufräumen, bevor Mama reinkommt."
"Don't cry, Jimmy," said the oldest brother. "We will figure something out. Let's just clean up this mess quickly before Mom comes in."

Gerade, als sie damit fertig waren, alles an Ort und Stelle zurückzustellen, kam ihre Mutter in die Küche gelaufen.
Just as the brothers finished putting everything back in its place, Jimmy's mother walked into the kitchen.

„Wir werden bald zu Mittag essen. Wo ist Jimmy?" Jimmy versteckte sich hinter seinen älteren Brüdern.
"We're going to eat lunch soon. Where's Jimmy?" Jimmy hid behind his older brothers.

„Äh, ähm…", stotterte sein mittlerer Bruder, während er überlegte, was er sagen sollte. Aber der ältere Bruder war sehr schlau.
"Uh, uh…," stuttered his middle brother while thinking of what to say. But the older brother was very smart.

„Mama, wenn jemand schnell groß und stark werden wollte, was müsste er tun?", fragte er.

"Mom, if someone wants to grow quickly and be tall and strong, what would he need to do?" he asked.

„Er muss sein Obst und Gemüse essen", antwortete sie. *„Sie enthalten viele Vitamine und Mineralien, die dem Körper helfen, schneller zu wachsen."*
"He needs to eat his fruits and vegetables," she answered. "They contain lots of vitamins and minerals that help the body grow faster."

„Ihr könnt euch jetzt an den Tisch setzen und ich werde Papa und Jimmy rufen", sagte ihre Mutter und verließ die Küche.
"Now, you can sit down at the table and I will call Dad and Jimmy," their mother said and walked out of the kitchen.

Der älteste Bruder drehte sich zu Jimmy um. „Schnell! Du musst dein Obst und Gemüse essen."
The oldest brother turned around to Jimmy. "Quick! You have to eat your fruits and vegetables."

„Auf keinen Fall!", schrie Jimmy. „Ich mag kein Obst oder Gemüse!"
"No way!" screamed Jimmy, "I don't even like fruits or vegetables!"

„Willst du für immer so bleiben?", fragte sein mittlerer Bruder.

"Do you want to stay this way forever then?" his middle brother asked.

„Natürlich nicht!", sagte Jimmy.

"Of course not!" replied Jimmy.

„Dann iss etwas Gemüse", sagte der älteste Bruder. „Vielleicht magst du es sogar."

"So eat some vegetables," said the oldest brother. "Maybe you'll even like them."

Er nahm eine Karotte aus der Schüssel auf dem Tisch und steckte sie Jimmy in den Mund.

He took a carrot from the bowl on the table and slipped it in Jimmy's mouth.

„Ähm….das ist süß und lecker", sagte Jimmy, als er mit seinen kräftigen weißen Zähnen seine Karotte kaute.

"Ummm...this is sweet and tasty," Jimmy said as he chewed his carrot with his strong, white teeth.

Plötzlich spürte er ein seltsames, kribbelndes Gefühl, das sich über seinen ganzen Körper ausbreitete - es war wie Zauberei. Seine Beine wurden stärker und er wurde sogar ein bisschen größer.

All of the sudden, he felt a strange tingly feeling spreading all over his body—it was just like magic. His legs got stronger, and he even became a little taller.

„Jimmy, schau! Du bist ein bisschen gewachsen!", schrie der älteste Bruder.

"Jimmy, look! You've grown a bit!" shouted the oldest brother happily.

Der mittlere Bruder gab Jimmy eine saftige Gurke aus der Schüssel. „Hier, iss etwas anderes", sagte er.

The middle brother gave Jimmy a juicy cucumber from the bowl. "Here, eat something else," he said.

Mit jedem Bissen fühlte Jimmy seinen Körper stärker und stärker werden. Er wuchs!

With every bite, he felt his body getting stronger and stronger. He was growing!

„Du bist endlich wieder du selbst", schrie der älteste Bruder und rannte zu ihm, um Jimmy zu umarmen.

"You're finally yourself again," the oldest brother shouted and ran over to hug Jimmy.

Sein mittlerer Bruder umarmte ihn auch. „Wie fühlst du dich jetzt?", fragte er.

His middle brother hugged him, too. "How are you feeling now?" he asked.

„Ich fühle mich toll und voller Energie", antwortete Jimmy. „Und wisst ihr was? Dieses Obst und Gemüse ist wirklich lecker! Ich hätte es eher probieren sollen!"

"I feel great and full of energy," Jimmy answered. "And you know what? These fruits and vegetables are really tasty. I should have tried them before!"

Alle drei Brüder fingen an, laut zu lachen und herumzuhüpfen.

All three brothers began to laugh loudly and jump around.

Ein paar Minuten später kamen Jimmys Eltern in die Küche.

A few minutes later, Jimmy's parents entered the kitchen.

"Toll, ihr seid hier", sagte Papa.

"Great, everyone's here," said Dad.

„Es freut mich, dass alle so gute Laune haben", sagte Mama. „Was für ein wundervoller Start für das Mittagessen! Vergesst nicht, eure Hände zu waschen!"

"I'm happy that everyone's in such a good mood," said Mom. "What a great way for us to start lunch! Don't forget to wash your hands!"

Die glückliche Familie saß um den großen Tisch herum und begann, all die leckeren Sachen darauf zu essen. Sogar Jimmy aß seinen ganzen Teller auf.

The entire happy family sat around the large table and began eating all the tasty things there. Even Jimmy finished his whole plateful.

Von diesem Tage an aß Jimmy gerne sein ganzes Obst und Gemüse. Manchmal aß er immer noch Süßigkeiten, aber nur ein paar und nur nach seinen Mahlzeiten.

From that day on, Jimmy liked eating all his fruits and vegetables. Sometimes, he still eats candy but only a little and only after his meals.

www.ingramcontent.com/pod-product-compliance
Lightning Source LLC
LaVergne TN
LVHW072104060526
838200LV00061B/4805